What makes Popcorn Pop?

TEXT BY
JANE PARKER RENICK
REBECCA L. GRAMBO
& TONY TALLARICO

ILLUSTRATIONS BY
TONY TALLARICO

Kidsbooks®

Manufactured in the United States of America

0406-1K

Visit us at **www.kidsbooks.com**

How many people live in the world?

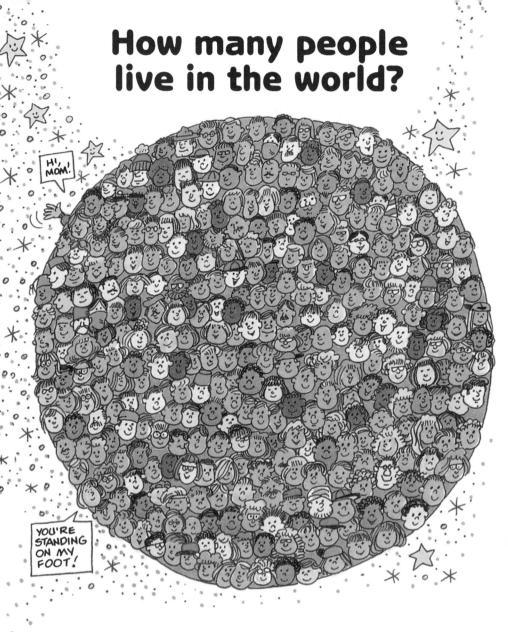

At the end of 2005, the population of the world was more than six and a half billion. By 2020, scientists estimate that eight billion people will inhabit Earth and by 2030 that number could grow to over nine billion.

What is the difference between a sea and an ocean?

Seas are smaller than oceans. A sea can be part of one of the four oceans (Atlantic, Pacific, Indian, and Arctic). The Caribbean Sea of North America, for instance, is in the Atlantic. Other seas, such as the Caspian Sea in Asia, are surrounded by land.

How tall is the world's tallest living tree?

A giant redwood in the Humboldt Redwoods State Park in California is the tallest tree on Earth. How tall is it? You could look out the top-floor window of a building 30 stories high—and still not see the top. At last measurement, in July, 2004, it was 370 feet tall!

What makes a skunk smell?

That ghastly spray is the skunk's best defense and, boy, does it work! No creature, human or beast, can stand being near a skunk with that odor. It comes from a fluid called musk which is produced and stored in a pair of glands under the animal's tail. A skunk can propel the spray about 10 feet!

When were comic books invented?

Comic books are single-square newspaper cartoons that have grown up. From single-square cartoons came comic strips, which are several squares long. The first comic book, as we know it, was *Funnies on Parade*, a one-time shot published in 1933. The first comic-book series was *Famous Funnies*, which first appeared in 1934. The first comic-book super-hero, Superman, landed on newsstands in 1939.

What is the Loch Ness Monster?

Now you see it, now you don't! In 1933, a couple claimed they saw a dinosaur-like monster in Loch Ness, a lake in Scotland. Three thousand sightings of "Nessie" have occurred since, but none of them has proven the creature's existence for sure!

Why do people snore?

If someone catches you snoring, blame your uvula (OOV-you-la). It's a small piece of flesh at the back of the throat that hangs down from the roof of the mouth. Sometimes air from the lungs causes the uvula to vibrate—and that's the snoring sound. It happens most often when you breathe through your mouth.

What is a jet stream?

Jet streams are Earth's fastest large-scale winds. A large-scale wind is a high current of air that blows over vast distances. About 30,000 to 35,000 feet above Earth's surface, large masses of cold air move in from the poles to clash with warmer air masses from the tropics. This creates the mighty rivers of wind known as jet streams.

HA-HA! HEE-HEE! HO-HO!

Why are feet so ticklish?

Nerve endings are what make us feel ticklish. And the more nerve endings there are in a particular spot, the more ticklish it is. Our feet have the most nerve endings—so they're the most ticklish of all!

How big is the biggest diamond in the world?

Diamonds, like other gems, are measured in carats. (Not carrots, those are for rabbits.) A carat weighs 0.2 grams. The largest fine quality, colorless diamond ever found was called "The Cullinan." It was mined in South Africa and weighed 3,106 carats. It was cut into 106 jewels and produced the finest, largest gemstone ever, weighing 530.2 carats.

What is octopus ink?

It's a smoke screen. When threatened, an octopus discharges a thick blackish or brownish inky fluid which is stored in its body. The ejected ink doesn't dissolve quickly. It floats in the water in a cloud shaped somewhat like an octopus. The idea is to confuse its enemies and cover its escape—and it works.

Who invented pizza?

Pizza was first cooked up in the kitchens of Naples, Italy, about 500 years ago. No one person created it. It was just something a lot of people ate around Naples. The Duke of Naples made pizza popular by adding a variety of toppings. Without cheese and tomato sauce toppings, pizza is just plain crusty dough.

Why can't I see in the dark?

The human eye uses light to see. Light bounces off your surroundings and into your eye through your pupil, the black hole at the center. A picture forms on your retina, the lining at the back of the eye. Your brain makes sense out of what you see. Without light, there is nothing to enter your retina and start the whole process going.

I DIDN'T KNOW THAT?!

What is ESP?

ESP stands for **E**xtra **S**ensory **P**erception. Regular sensory perception is the way we see the world through our five senses—sight, hearing, smell, taste, and touch. But "extra" goes beyond that and includes having an awareness of information NOT gained through the senses. That could include having dreams that come true, hearing the voices of dead people, or getting a strong feeling about something that is going to happen in the future.

Why is it considered unlucky to open an umbrella indoors?

Umbrellas were first used by African royalty to shield themselves from the hot rays of the sun god. To open one in the shade insulted the god. To open one indoors must have been worse, probably punishable by the god. Today, we think of it as just plain unlucky.

HOW DO CLOUDS FORM?

Millions of water droplets together form clouds. They start out as *water vapor*, the evaporated water that rises from lakes, oceans, rivers, and plants. Water vapor cools as it rises into the air and, as the temperature drops, it changes to liquid. These masses of tiny water droplets form clouds. When the clouds get too heavy, they fall to Earth as rain. They flow into lakes and rivers...and the whole process begins all over again.

ARE THERE ANY REAL CASTLES IN THE WORLD?

Think of your house as your castle. The kings, queens, and nobles of the Middle Ages did. Their castles were their homes, the places where they lived. But castles were also symbols of their power, and fortresses against rivals who might try to make war on them. These grand homes were built between the ninth and the fifteenth centuries all over Europe. Many have been preserved—and you can visit them. They're mostly hotels or museums now.

WHAT IS STONEHENGE?

Stonehenge is a mystery—on a grand scale. An enormous ancient monument, Stonehenge was built in southern England over 3,000 years ago. The monument consists of many large stones, some weighing up to 100,000 pounds, arranged in circular patterns. It may have been used to observe the movements of the sun and moon—and then to create calendars. No one really knows.

Why can I drink something really hot, but if I spilled the same thing on myself, it would burn?

Your mouth has air-conditioning! As you sip a hot liquid, air comes into your mouth along with it and cools the drink. Your saliva mixes in and cools it further. But hot stuff on your skin is just plain hot!

Who wrote the song **"Happy Birthday to You"**?

The Hill girls, Mildred and Patty, wrote "Good Morning to You" in 1893. The song was not a big hit until someone changed the words. No one knows exactly who made the change. There aren't many words, but for birthdays, four is all you need:

Happy Birthday to You!

9

What's the difference between a dolphin and a porpoise?

WE'RE MAMMAL COUSINS.

Their facial structure and body size. Both are mammals, not fish, and have to breathe above water. Both are related to whales, but are smaller. Dolphins can grow to 12 feet in length and have a beak. Porpoises are beakless and are usually between three and six feet long.

-46 -47 -48 -49-
50-51 -52-53-
54-55-56-

WHAT'S THE DIFFERENCE BETWEEN AN INSECT AND A SPIDER ?

Look out for legs. Spiders have eight. Insects have six. Also check out the antennae. Insects have them and spiders don't. Up close (if you dare), look at the number of body parts. Insects have three. Spiders have two. And if the animal is hanging by a thread, it's a spider. Spiders make silk. Insects don't.

How fast do a hummingbird's wings beat?

Faster than you can see. Hummingbirds, the smallest feathered creatures on the planet, are also the fastest wing-beaters. The beating is so speedy it looks like a blur. With a slow motion camera, it can almost be counted—50 to 75 beats per second! Hummingbirds can even fly backwards, something no other bird can do.

WHY DO ZEBRAS AND TIGERS HAVE STRIPES?

Camouflage—to help them hide. If a zebra or a tiger were in your backyard, you'd know it. But if you were in their neighborhood, you might miss them. Striped coats are hard to see in the light and dark shadows of forests and grasslands. This helps to keep them safe from predators. Now you see them. Now you don't!

The vibration of shell-like rings on the end of its tail. The rattle is made up of dry, hard pieces of unshed skin. As the snake grows, the number of rings increases. So, the louder the rattle, the bigger the snake. The snake will shake its rattles to tell an intruder to..."Take off!"

What makes a rattlesnake's tail rattle?

I'M GOING OUT!

Why does a match light up?

In a word—friction. Matches were the accidental discovery of John Walker, a chemist. In 1827, he was trying to produce a burnable material for shotguns. His first match was a stick he was using to stir a mixture of chemicals. It burst into flames when he scraped it against a stone floor to clean off the end.

How often can we see an eclipse of the sun?

Solar eclipses can be seen only from certain parts of Earth's surface—different places at different times. If you're willing to travel, however, the average number of eclipses is two to five times a year. Five is highly unusual. The last time Earth experienced five solar eclipses in a year was 1935; it won't happen again until 2206!

When were roller skates invented?

Talk about an entrance! To introduce his invention, Joseph Merlin of Huy, Belgium, roller-skated into a ballroom playing the violin. That was in 1759. Unfortunately, he didn't know how to stop and crashed into a full-length mirror, breaking his violin.

Who invented money?

The first piece of metal to be considered a coin was invented in Lydia, Turkey, around 670 B.C. But the idea of money took shape over a long time. People traded ten chickens for a cow, or a basket of berries for six ears of corn. But what if the person with the berries wanted wheat instead of corn? Or what if the owner of the berries left them at home? Eventually, it made sense to have something that always had the same value and was easy to carry. And that something was money.

WHAT IS GLASS MADE OF?

OOPS!

Glass starts out being soft and syrupy. It's a mixture of sand, soda, and limestone melted together at high temperatures. In this state it can be shaped into the glass objects we see around us. Various minerals can be added to make different colored glass. Then, the "syrup" is cooled, heated, and cooled again in a process that makes it hard.

How many stars are in the Milky Way galaxy?

About 200 billion, including our sun. Those billions of stars are arrayed in a vast spiral that is about 100,000 light-years in diameter. The Milky Way's many stars are constantly moving, rotating around the galaxy's center. How fast is that rotation? Our sun, which is on one of the galaxy's outer arms, takes 200 million to 230 million years to make one complete rotation!

What makes popcorn pop?

Every kernel of corn has a tiny droplet of water in it. Heat the kernel, and the water turns to steam. Steam takes up more space than water, so it presses against the walls of the kernel. The corn expands and expands and...explodes! Popppppp!

WHY DO I GET THE HICCUPS?

It all starts with your diaphragm, the big muscle below your lungs. Usually, the diaphragm works smoothly, expanding and contracting your lungs. But if it gets irritated, perhaps by eating too quickly, it pulls down sharply. Air whooshes into your lungs...Hic! To keep too much air from entering your lungs, a small flap at the top of your windpipe snaps shut...Cup!

STAND CLEAR FOR POPPING POPCORN

What is the most powerful muscle in my body?

Your jaw muscle—and it's because exercise makes muscles stronger! Talking and chewing exercise this muscle more than any other.

WHAT DO INSECTS EAT?

That depends on the insect. Some, such as potato beetles, eat leaves. Termites eat wood. Some insects, including bees, butterflies, and male mosquitoes, suck nectar from flowers. Female mosquitoes suck blood. Many other insects eat other insects. Some, such as water striders, even eat others of their own kind!

I BET YOU CAN'T EAT ONLY ONE!

How do you make potato chips?

Deep-fat frying is the good old-fashioned way. Slice some potatoes as thinly as possible. Soak them in cold water for two hours, changing the water twice. Drain them and dry them carefully with paper towels. In a deep pot, bring some cooking oil to a high heat. Drop the potato slices into the hot oil. Shake and stir, cooking them until they're golden. Drain them on paper towels and eat. Delicious! If you want to try making your own potato chips, ask an adult for some help!

IS THAT MY BEEPER?

How do whales talk?

They sing! Or to be specific, male humpback whales do. The songs of the humpbacks are a form of communication much stronger than the human voice. Underwater, whales send messages heard several miles away. Whales make sounds with a system of tubes and air sacs around their blowholes. Squeaks and whistles and strange moaning are what whale songs sound like to humans. The songs of male humpbacks have been taped. People listen to these recordings as they would any other kind of music.

Why do flamingos stand on one leg?

Standing on one leg and then the other helps a flamingo conserve body heat and energy. It also allows each limb to dry and keep warm.

Do animals use tools?

Some do. The woodpecker finch of the Galapagos Islands uses a tool to dig insects out of holes. The bird uses a cactus spine, which it holds in its beak. Apes use twigs and blades of grass to hunt insects. Seabirds use rocks. They drop clams and other hard-shelled sea creatures against the hard rocks to split open their shells.

HOW DOES AN ELECTRIC GUITAR WORK?

Play an electric guitar and you're actually producing sound with an amplifier and a loudspeaker, not a set of strings. Each metal string is attached to a pick-up, which is a small coil of wire with magnets set in it. The pick-up sends an electrical signal to the amplifier, then to the loudspeaker, and right to your audience.

What is Silly Putty™?

A substance that bounces, stretches, and picks up ink when pressed against newsprint. Its inventor saw no practical use for the odd stuff, but a businessman named Peter Hodgson recognized its potential as a toy. Hodgson named it Silly Putty and, in 1949, started selling one-ounce balls of it in colorful plastic eggs. It was a great success: Children around the world still play with it today.

What's the difference between a tortoise and a turtle?

WE'RE COUSINS!

A tortoise lives on land. It has clubbed feet like an elephant and a shell that is high-domed and thick. The largest tortoises can be 500 pounds. The turtle is a water creature with legs that resemble flippers. Leatherback turtles, by far the largest turtle, can grow to eight feet and weigh 1,500 pounds!

HOW DO YOU MAKE CARTOONS?

Bugs Bunny bites a carrot. Beauty kisses the Beast. The movement looks natural, but it's really made up of hundreds of *still* drawings. These drawings are flipped very fast in a row—24 per second! The speed gives the illusion of movement. How are the drawings "flipped"? —by using a special high-speed camera. Today, computers also help make the still drawings "move."

How does a caterpillar turn into a butterfly?

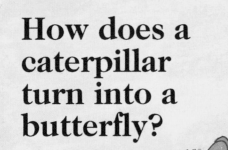

It's not a miracle . . . it's *metamorphosis*, which means "change of form." A butterfly begins life as an egg, which grows into a caterpillar. After a period of maturing, a hard shell called a *chrysalis* develops over the caterpillar. Inside, the creature's body gradually changes. The shell breaks open, and out comes a lovely butterfly.

WHAT'S IT LIKE AT THE BOTTOM OF THE OCEAN?

The deeper you go, the darker it gets. Many fish who live at 2,000 feet or deeper have their own flashlights. They are *luminous*—they glow with light-producing cells. This light helps them get around in the blackness and attract prey. Other fish are blind—since they can't see down there, they never developed functioning eyes. Most of all, it's *cold* at the bottom—sometimes as cold as 28 degrees Fahrenheit.

HI!

What was the first tool?

In 1976, scientists found a chopper made of stone in Ethiopia in Africa. They believe that the object was made by early humans around 2.7 million years ago. It would have been handy for digging, scraping, or hacking.

How do evergreens stay green all year?

It's due to the shape of their leaves—or needles. Trees take up water through their roots. The water evaporates into the air through their leaves. Trees with flat, broad leaves lose a lot of water. In winter, when the ground is frozen, these trees shed their leaves to hold on to their water supply. But evergreens have needle-like leaves with a thick, waxy covering. These needles don't lose much moisture, so they remain on the tree. After a few years, they fall off, but new ones grow in at the same time, so the tree is *ever green!*

How can a parrot talk?

By repeating the "nonsense" sounds it hears over and over and over again. When a parrot says "Polly wants a cracker," it doesn't have a cracker in mind. The bird can't understand what it's saying. But it can learn to make the sounds by practicing. In the same way, you could learn to say a few sentences in a foreign language you didn't know.

I DON'T LIKE CRACKERS!

How do bees make honey?

It all starts with nectar, the sugary juice of flowers that honeybees bring back to the hive. In the hive, worker bees add important enzymes (or chemicals) from their bodies to the nectar and deposit it in the honeycombs. Then, special bees fan this nectar with their wings. The heat of the hive and the fanning make some of the water in the nectar evaporate, and turn it into honey.

How does a sprouting seed know which way is up?

WHICH WAY IS UP?

Gravity gives the seed directions. Tiny nodules in the growing tips of seeds respond to gravity so that the roots are pulled downward. That way, the shoots will always point up.

How old is the universe?

Fifteen billion years is the estimate. The big mystery is how the universe began. One important theory is the Big Bang. Some scientists believe that all matter was once a single mass. Then an enormous explosion sent pieces flying off into space, creating galaxies and planets and stars. The theory says that the galaxies are all still moving away from each other because of the force of that explosion billions of years ago. But other scientists think things have always been pretty much the same.

What is a meteor?

Meteors have more than one name, just like people. Particles of matter or pieces of rock that fall through space are called meteoroids. If they burn up in the Earth's atmosphere, they are called meteors. Most of them burn into nothing and are never seen again, but if they survive and hit the ground, they become meteorites and form big craters where they land.

WHY DO WE SNEEZE?

Your nose knows. Anything that gets in your nose, like dust or germs, is something your body doesn't want. You sneeze to get rid of it. The big A-Choo! is air from your lungs that comes up, shoots rapidly through your nose, and clears it.

A-A-CHOO!

Who was Mozart?

Wolfgang Amadeus Mozart was one of the world's youngest musicians. He was born in Austria in 1756 and composed his first piece for a full symphony orchestra at the age of five! He also performed. During his lifetime, he created many symphonies, concertos, and operas—some of the most beautiful music ever written. And he lived only 35 years.

Why is a four-leaf clover considered LUCKY?

Legends about the four-leaf clover go all the way back to Adam and Eve. It is said that Eve took a four-leaf clover when she was sent from the Garden of Eden. A piece of green from the world's first garden spot must be something rare and wonderful—special enough to bring good luck.

Why does the sky change color from red at dawn to blue during the day?

The sun's white light is actually made up of many colors—red, orange, yellow, green, blue, indigo, and violet. When light comes through the atmosphere and is scattered by dust particles, the various different shades of light are separated. Which one we see depends on how thick the layer of dust is and where the sun may be. During the day, when the sun is high in the sky, blue light is scattered the most. At dusk and dawn, when the sun is near the horizon, we see it through a much thicker layer of dust. The red and orange light comes through most, and the sky gets fiery.

WHO INVENTED NUMBERS?

Numbers are really ideas. We can't see them, so we create signs or symbols to represent them. The concept of numbers, and the symbols to represent them, developed when people needed to count things. Different civilizations used different kinds of numbers. The 1, 2, 3 type of numbers we use are called Arabic numerals. They were probably invented by the Hindus in India about 1,400 years ago. But it isn't the oldest system. The Babylonians invented a number system about 3,500 years ago.

Nature didn't do it. Manufacturers give drinks the fizz that tickles your taste buds. First, they force carbon dioxide into the drink under pressure and seal the bottle or can. The gas stays in the liquid until you open the drink. Then . . . *whoosh! hiss!* . . . the carbon dioxide escapes. Where does it go? It's in the bubbles.

WHAT IS GRAVITY?

The big pull. Gravity is the force at the center of a planet that attracts other objects to it. The Earth's force of gravity keeps our feet on the ground. Gravity actually holds the universe together, too. The sun's gravity keeps the planets in their orbits. Without it, the Earth would shoot off into space.

HOW LONG HAVE ESCALATORS BEEN GOING UP AND DOWN?

About a century. Coney Island, New York, had the world's first escalator in 1896. In London in 1911, people were worried about putting their feet on that city's first moving stairs. So a man with a wooden leg was hired to take the ride and show that if a man with one leg could do it, the two-legged types had nothing to fear.

HOW DOES A FLYING FISH FLY?

Not like a bird. These small fish (the largest is about a foot and a half) propel themselves into the air with their tails and glide. Fear makes them do it. If a bigger fish is chasing them, they flap their tails, pick up speed, and leap out of the water. Then they spread their front fins and sail on the breeze—up to 20 miles per hour.

What happens when I dream?

You "see" your dreams with your eyes. Dream sleep is called REM sleep for Rapid Eye Movement because your eyes move behind your closed lids as if you were scanning a picture. Scientists think that dreaming is a way of sorting out and storing the happenings of the day.

Who invented indoor plumbing?

Someone we should all thank. On the Mediterranean island of Crete, a system was installed 4,000 years ago. Indoor plumbing requires pipes that bring water into the house and drainage pipes that take waste out. The flush toilet was invented by Sir John Harrington in 1589, but didn't reach its present form until the 1800s.

What is QUICKSAND ?

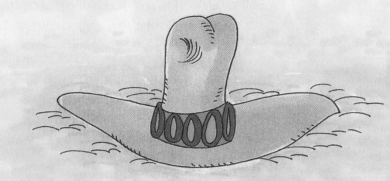

A very thick liquid that is formed when water flows through and mixes with sand. Quicksand appears to be firm enough to walk on, but any object that steps into or lands on the soft mixture will sink into it. You can't "stand" vertically in water and expect to keep your head above it. The same is true of quicksand.

What makes the Leaning Tower of Pisa lean?

The Leaning Tower of Pisa in northern Italy is a church bell tower. Its construction began in 1173, but was soon halted when the builders realized the 10-foot foundation wasn't deep enough to keep the tower from tilting in the soft soil. The 180-foot tower, weighing 16,000 tons, was finally completed 200 years later. To keep it from toppling over, the people of Pisa have repeatedly gone in and reinforced the foundation. But they haven't dared try to straighten the tower!

EVERYBODY — PULL TOGETHER!

UGH!

OOFF!

IT'S NOT MOVING

Why do people have straight, wavy, or curly hair?

As a strand of hair grows, it squeezes through a tiny hole called a follicle. The shape of a person's follicles makes hair straight, wavy, or curly. Think of a toothpaste tube—if the opening weren't round, but shaped like a square or a star instead, the stream of toothpaste would look completely different. Straight hair grows out of round follicles, waves from oval follicles, and tight, round curls spring from square follicles!

Why do salmon and other fish swim upstream?

THIS WAY

Because they return to where they were born when they are ready to breed. And that can be a long way—sometimes thousands of miles. Salmon are born in rivers and streams and then travel to sea to live as adults. But instinct helps them find their way home. They swim against the current and even jump over waterfalls trying to find the exact spot where they were born.

What causes EARTHQUAKES?

THIS IS A GOOD TIME TO MAKE A MILKSHAKE!

The problem is underground. Pressure inside the Earth causes giant plates of rocks in the Earth's crust to shove against one another. When these rock plates collide, the Earth's surface cracks, and the ground shakes. The shock waves carry the shudders for miles, and the Earth *quakes*.

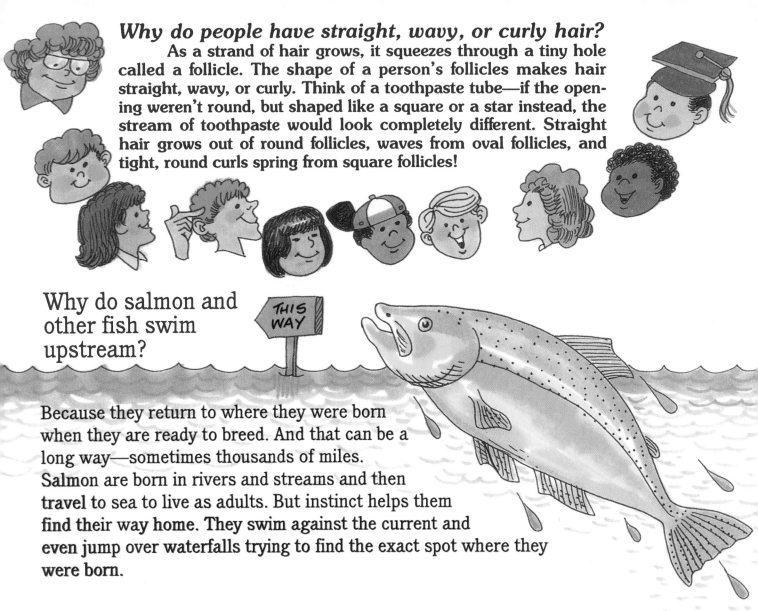

Who started April Fool's Day?

Silly days for practical jokes are found all around the world. Perhaps the day started with the French, who once began the new year on the first of April. In 1564, when the new calendar began the year with January 1, some people resisted. They were considered April fools.

What was the first movie?

In Paris, France, in 1895, Louis and Auguste Lumiere showed the first moving picture, a short film of workers leaving a factory. The first movie with a story was Edwin Porter's *The Great Train Robbery* in 1903. It was a sensation, but silent. In 1927, *The Jazz Singer* was the first full-length movie with sound.

TODAY, THE TRAIN WOULD BE LATE!!

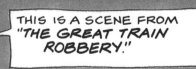

THIS IS A SCENE FROM *"THE GREAT TRAIN ROBBERY."*

WHAT KEEPS MY BONES TOGETHER?

Ligaments. When two bones come together at a joint, like your elbow or your knee, they are not directly attached. Tough, stretchy straps called ligaments surround them. They join the joints. If you injure a ligament badly the joint could slip apart.

HOW MANY HAIRS ARE ON A PERSON'S HEAD?

I THINK I NEED A HAIRCUT!

The average is about 125,000 hairs, but they would be very hard to count. Head hair is always falling out and growing in. About 50 to 75 hairs fall out each day.

WHAT GIVES MY EYES THEIR COLOR?

The iris. The iris surrounds the pupil, the opening at the center, and controls the amount of light that passes through the hole. The back of the iris has pigment—called melanin—that protects it from light. This is the color we see. If you have blue or green-colored eyes, the iris has small amounts of melanin. Larger amounts of the pigment give you brown or hazel eyes.

WHAT ARE TEARS FOR?

Tears are cleaning fluid for the eye. They come from the lacrimal glands, which sit above the outer edge of each eye. And tears keep coming. Every time you blink, they cover your eye and wash away dirt and germs. When you cry, tears may help you get rid of extra chemicals that build up in your body.

WHAT CAUSES AN ALLERGY?

A mistake. Your body has an army to defend you against germs. The main soldiers are white cells, which create antibodies to attack specific germs. But sometimes the white cells act as if harmless foreign substances, like dust or pollen, are dangerous. They cause your nose to run, your eyes to tear, and your skin to itch.

THIS IS NOT MY DAY!

SNIFF-SNIFF!

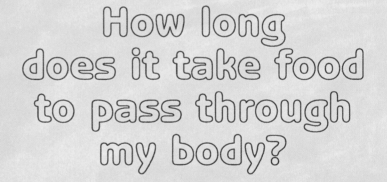

How many different kinds of rocks are there?

ONLY THREE?

Even though rocks are everywhere, they are all variations of only three basic kinds. *Sedimentary* rocks, like limestone, are formed near the surface of the Earth when erosion causes sand, pebbles, and shells to get buried in layers. *Igneous* rocks, like granite, were once liquid lava which cooled to hardness. *Metamorphic* rocks, like slate, are sedimentary or igneous rocks changed by underground heat and pressure.

What are sponges made of?

Sponges are animals that live on the bottom of the ocean and never move (there is one fresh-water variety). Some have beautiful and fantastic colors. Sponges have a skeleton, cells that form chambers, and whip-like threads called *flagella* to capture tiny plants and animals for food.

How long does it take food to pass through my body?

About a day. Eat a burger today and it's gone tomorrow. Digestion—the breaking up of food into chemicals the body can use—begins with the saliva in the mouth, continues in the stomach, the small intestines, and then the large intestines. Your intestines, one long tube all coiled up, can be up to 30 feet long! They absorb nutrients and water from food, as it moves on down the line.

WHO WAS THE FIRST PERSON TO GET PIERCED EARS?

Earrings are ornaments of ancient Middle Eastern and East Indian civilizations. Both men and women wore them. Gold and silver, flowers and birds, pearls and gems were all worn on one ear or two depending on the style of the day. The Greeks even hung gold earrings on statues of goddesses.

WHY CAN'T I BLOW BUBBLES WITH REGULAR GUM?

Trees have the secret ingredient. All gum contains gum base, sweeteners, and wood resin. Bubble gum has more wood resin, which provides the glue and the stretch. Without as much resin, regular gum isn't elastic enough to expand and hold the bubble you blow.

When was the first car invented?

In 1770, Nicolas Cugnot, a French soldier, built a steam engine that travelled about three miles per hour. It was so big that this "self-propelled road vehicle" was impossible to steer. In 1862, J. J. Etienne Lenoir, of Paris, took his carriage with an internal combustion engine for its first ride: six miles in three hours at an average speed of two miles per hour.

HOW BIG WAS THE BIGGEST ICEBERG EVER?

Bigger than some countries! In 1956, an iceberg was sighted that was 208 miles long and 60 miles wide. That's about the size of Belgium. Only a small part of this ice monster was seen above water. Most icebergs hide nine-tenths of their size under the surface.

THAT'S A LOT OF ICE!

What causes twins?

"Identical" twins are born when one fertilized egg splits into two. They are the same sex and look alike. "Fraternal" twins are born when two eggs are fertilized. They can be a boy and a girl, or both the same sex. They usually resemble each other no more than any other siblings.

YOU LOOK LIKE ME!

YOU LOOK LIKE ME!

Why do plants turn to face the light?

Not to get a tan. Their leaves, which contain chlorophyll, create food in combination with light. So they must face the sun. They also have growth substances, which gather in the stem cells that do not face the light. This creates more growth on the shaded side than on the sunny side, which causes the plant to bend toward the light.

What is the Great Sphinx and the pyramids?

Along with the Egyptian pyramids, the Great Sphinx is one of the oldest stone structures in the world. The 4,500-year-old sphinx represents the god Horus, who guarded temples and tombs. It has the body of a lion and the face of the pharaoh, or king, who built it to guard his pyramid. Slaves and ancient Egyptians built the pyramids as tombs for their pharaohs. It took tens of thousands of men over 20 years to erect the largest, the 480-foot Great Pyramid built around 2600 B.C. There are still over 80 pyramids in Egypt today.

HAVE YOU SEEN A MUMMY?

HOW DOES A SPIDER SPIN A WEB?

Spiders manufacture silk in their bodies—but not the kind of silk we wear. At the end of their abdomens, they have *spinnerets*, which produce silk threads for web building. The silk is elastic and sticky. The spider fastens a thread to an anchoring point like a leaf or twig and draws out more line. As the web grows the spider can walk on it like a tightrope and attach lines in any design.

I LIKE THIS DESIGN!

Where was the world's largest birthday party?

In Buffalo, New York, on July 4, 1991, about 75,000 people sang "Happy Birthday" during a Friendship Festival that's held every year. Buffalo, not far from Canada, was celebrating the birthdays of both countries.

I HAVE SEEDS!

I DON'T!

I WASN'T INVITED TO THAT BIRTHDAY PARTY!

What's the difference between fruits and vegetables?

Seeds make the difference. Any fleshy part of a plant that grows from a flower is called its "fruit." If this part contains seeds, like an orange, an apple, a peach, or even a tomato, it's considered a fruit. If it has no seeds, like broccoli or lettuce or carrots, it's considered a vegetable.

Who was Queen Elizabeth I?

Queen Elizabeth I was England's queen from 1558 to 1603. She brought peace and prosperity to her devoted subjects, who called her "Good Queen Bess." She never married or shared her reign, and during her era—the Elizabethan Age—literature, drama, and music flourished. What a grand time it was!

Why is the sea salty?

There's salt in there. The salt content of an ocean is 3.5% by weight. The salt originates in rocks on the edges of the sea and in rivers and streams. Through the constant wetting and drying, the salt dissolves into the water and collects in the oceans.

I WASN'T INVITED TO THAT BIRTHDAY PARTY EITHER!

HOW DID PEOPLE CLEAN THEIR TEETH BEFORE TOOTHBRUSHES?

The natural way—twigs. People picked a good-tasting twig, chewed one end until it shredded, and used the "bristles." Or, they dipped their fingers in salt and rubbed their teeth. Three hundred years ago wooden-handled, hog-bristled toothbrushes were invented. In some places, they are still used.

... AND I DON'T NEED BATTERIES!

What makes a firefly light up?

Other fireflies! Fireflies (also called lightning bugs) blink their lights in a code that tells what species they are, whether they are male or female, and whether they are ready to mate. The light, produced by a chemical reaction in a special organ in the firefly's abdomen, may also serve as a warning.

... AND I SEE MY DENTIST TWICE A YEAR!

HOW MUCH DOES THE EARTH WEIGH?

5,972,000,000,000,000,000,000 tons (or 5.972 sextillion tons). And if that's not big enough for you, thousands of tons of cosmic dust and meteorites add to the Earth's weight every year.

WHAT'S THE DIFFERENCE BETWEEN A CAMEL AND A DROMEDARY?

One hump or two. There are two types of camels. Bactrian camels have two humps. The dromedary is a one-humped Arabian camel especially bred for riding and racing. These long-legged beasts can run about 10 miles an hour and travel as far as 100 miles a day.

WHAT IS THE OLDEST TREE IN THE WORLD?

A bristlecone pine on Mt. Wheeler in Nevada, was found to be 5,100 years old. The *inside* of a tree, not the outside, reveals its age. The number of rings seen on a tree stump or cut log tells the tree's age. Each ring is about a year's growth of wood cells.

THAT'S NOT A MEMBER OF MY FAMILY!

HOW DOES A SUBMARINE WORK?

Ballast is the key. It controls the weight of a ship. A submarine uses seawater kept in ballast tanks. The tanks are filled with water to make the ship heavier when it dives. To make the submarine lighter when it wants to surface, the water is forced out of the tanks by compressed air. Mechanical fins called hydroplanes direct the boat upward and downward.

AT LEAST I DON'T HAVE DANDRUFF!

WHY DO WE HAVE
H A I R ?

It used to be our coat. Prehistoric humans had hair all over their body to keep warm. Today, our eyebrows, eyelashes, and the hair in our nose and ears helps keep out dust. But what about the rest? We still have fine hair over most parts of our body—5 million hairs is the average for both men and women. But scientists don't know exactly why.

WHAT MAKES SNOW?

First the temperature has to be below freezing. Then a drop of water vapor may form a crystal around a particle of dust in the atmosphere. Some crystals stick together and form snowflakes heavy enough to fall to Earth. All snowflakes are different. The individual crystals are the same, but no two combinations are identical.

How many species of bats are there?

So many that it's hard to keep count. About 900 to 1,000 different species have been identified. Bats live in almost every part of the globe, except in very cold places, such as the Arctic, sub-Arctic, and Antarctic. How many individual bats are there? That is impossible to say, but some experts estimate that there are hundreds of millions of bats per species!

THAT'S A LOT OF WATERING!

HOW MANY DIFFERENT PLANTS ARE THERE IN THE WORLD?

More than we know. About 350,000 species of plants are known, but new ones are constantly being discovered. Plants range from algae to orchids to giant sequoia trees, and they're a hardy bunch. They've been on the planet for 3 billion years. Animal life didn't join them until about 600 million years ago.

WHAT'S THE DIFFERENCE BETWEEN A WHITE EGG AND A BROWN EGG?

It's in the chicken. Some breeds of chickens lay white eggs and some brown. The eggs fry, scramble, boil, and taste the same.

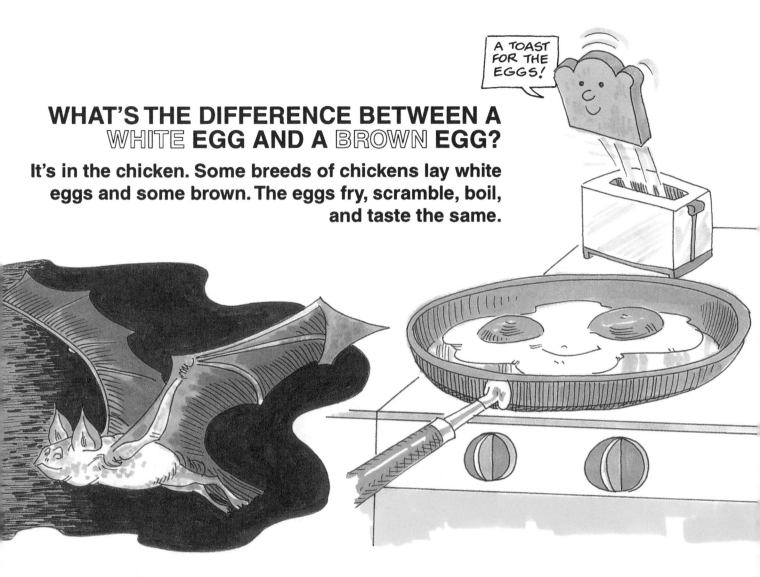

A TOAST FOR THE EGGS!

WHY CAN'T I TASTE ANYTHING WHEN I HAVE A COLD?

Because your nose is stuffed. Both your nose and your tongue have special cells that send messages to the brain about smells and tastes. In tasting, they work together. So, when you have a cold and your nose is lined with mucus, your smell cells are not getting the news that your tongue is tasting an orange. It's the pits.

WHAT'S THE MOST BEAUTIFUL PAINTING IN THE WORLD?

First, what's beautiful? Beauty in Los Angeles might not be the same in Timbuktu. Where you live changes how you feel about what's beautiful. And what *you* think is beautiful is probably different from a friend's idea of beauty. Beauty is personal. The painting considered to be one of the world's most beautiful, most famous, and most expensive (worth at least $100 million) is the "Mona Lisa." It was painted between 1503 and 1507 by Leonardo da Vinci.

I DID IT!

How many ants are in an ant colony?

That depends on the type of ant—and there are about 15,000 different kinds! But most ants are *social* insects that live in groups. Some colonies have only 10 ants and others have hundreds of thousands. Some nests are "hills," others are underground, and still others are built from leaves or found in wood. Wherever they live, ants will usually come out if you have a picnic.

I'M AN ANT AND AN UNCLE!

WHY DO PEOPLE HAVE DIFFERENT COLOR SKINS?

The difference is only skin deep. Melanin is the substance in the skin that produces darker shades. Since melanin protects the skin from the sun, more cells are created when we are exposed to the sun, and the skin becomes darker. The theory is that, in ancient times, people who lived in sunny climates were darker skinned, and those that lived in colder areas were fair. People today have inherited the color of their ancestors.

WHAT WOULD HAPPEN IF ALL THE *ICE* IN THE WORLD MELTED?

I HAD BETTER LEARN TO SWIM!

Some people would have to move. The seas would rise about 200 feet and the coasts of continents would gradually disappear under water. Floods in America would claim major centers like New York and San Fransisco. But don't panic. Scientists say the melting will happen, but not for thousands of years.

WHY DO MAGNETS ATTRACT?

Iron contains millions of tiny magnets called domains. Usually they are pointed in different directions and are not magnetized. A magnetized metal has all of its domains pointing in the same direction. All magnets have two poles, north and south, that pull iron and steel objects toward them, into their *magnetic field.* They only attract their opposites, north to south and south to north.

Why does hot water clean better than cold water?

It heats things up. Whatever's stuck on you dissolves better in heat. Soap grabs grease better in heat. And bacteria (tiny organisms that may carry disease) die in heat. Heat cleans things up.

HOW DO SNAKES MOVE IF THEY DON'T HAVE LEGS?

With a combination of muscles, scales, and an amazingly flexible spine. Snakes have belly scales, which grip the ground like tractor treads while their muscles pull their bodies forward. The spine is responsible for the snake's trademark curvy slither.

I WAS WONDERING ABOUT THAT MYSELF!

HOW IS PAPER MADE?

THIS IS GENUINE 100% PAPER!

It all starts with wood. Cut, ground up, mashed, watered, bleached, pressed, rolled out, and dried, wood becomes paper. Logs are ground up and combined with water and chemicals into a mixture called pulp. Shredded rags, glue, and coloring are added to make some papers. Then the pulp is dried and pressed into giant rolls.

What's my funny bone?

It's not humorous . . . it's *humerus*. That's your funny-bone's real name. It connects with the bones of your fore-arm at the elbow, a place where there are a bunch of sensitive nerves. When you whack that spot, it's no joke.

WHAT'S SO FUNNY?

WHO WAS THE FIRST PERSON IN SPACE?

When Russian Cosmonaut Yuri Alekseyevich Gagarin took off on April 12, 1961, he was the first person to leave the Earth in a satellite. He was up there alone for 108 minutes. Before returning, he traveled 17,560 miles. Although unafraid, Yuri must have been in a hurry.

?

HI!

WHY DO I FEEL DIZZY WHEN I SPIN AROUND?

You're making waves in your ears. Inside your ears are three semicircular canals filled with liquid. The ends of these tubes have nerves in a jelly-like substance that tell your brain your head's position. When your head spins, the liquid rocks and the jelly rolls. If you stop suddenly, everything keeps moving for a moment. *That's* when you feel dizzy.

SHE'S MAKING ME DIZZY JUST WATCHING HER !!!

COME ON DOWN!

WHAT ANIMAL GATHERS IN THE LARGEST GROUP?

The seal. Each year about 1.5 million Alaskan fur seals gather on the Pribilof Islands off the coast of Alaska to breed. The result: 500,000 baby seals.

HOW DOES A PARACHUTE WORK?

Perfectly . . . or else! When brave men and women jump out of airplanes, they pull a cord, and a canopy, or parachute, opens above them. This umbrella-shaped cloth resists the air, counteracts the jumper's weight, and slows the fall. When the person hits the ground, the force is about the same as a long jump.

HOW MUCH WATER IS THERE IN A WATERMELON?

Ninety-three percent! That means a 10-pound watermelon has 9.3 pounds of water. Is it a fruit or a drink? A fruit drink!

I'M A STAR!

WE'RE STARS, TOO!

I'M FALLING.

ME, TOO.

WHAT'S THE DIFFERENCE BETWEEN A COMET AND A SHOOTING STAR?

Shooting stars are meteors that burn up in the Earth's atmosphere. Comets consist of mostly frozen gas, ice, and dust. Unlike planets, neither circles the sun, but they do orbit in space. Comets have fiery tails, which we see when they pass the Earth. The heat of the sun turns the ice into gas, which forms the comet's tail as it escapes.

THIS IS A GREAT PLACE TO SKATE BOARD!

What is the Great Wall of China?

One of the largest and most ambitious building projects ever undertaken. Over several centuries, beginning in the 7th century B.C., the people of ancient China built the wall to keep out invaders.

The most important work was led by Shih Huangdi, who became emperor in 221 B.C. He united China's many warring territories into one nation. To defend it, he had the wall's many parts joined into one continous defensive line. Not counting branches and side sections, it is nearly 4,160 miles long!

WHAT'S THE HOTTEST PLACE IN THE UNITED STATES?

The hottest temperature ever recorded in the United States was 134°F in Death Valley, California, on July 10, 1913. It was not a cool summer. The thermometer hit 120°F for 43 days in a row.

136°

THIS IS **HOT!**

0°

WHAT CAUSES A TORNADO?

A tornado forms in storm clouds when masses of hot, humid air rise and begin to rotate. The rotating funnel cloud can extend down to the ground and destroy everything in its path. (The quicker the spin— some rotate faster than 300 miles an hour—the more powerful the tornado.) A tornado's funnel, which can be from 50 feet to a mile wide, travels with a storm cloud at an average speed of 30 to 40 miles an hour.

WHEN WAS THE CHOCOLATE BAR INVENTED?

In 1811. A chocolate drink was first brought to Europe from the Aztecs of Mexico in the 1500s. Three hundred years later, Francois-Louis Cailler of Switzerland manufactured the first chocolate in bars. How many things can you think of that have chocolate in them?

HOW DOES A PLANE STAY UP IN THE AIR?

SO, THAT'S HOW I FLY!

I DON'T HAVE WINGS!

Power and lift. Power comes from the engines. Lift comes from the wings, which are called airfoils. Airfoils are rounded on top, flat on the bottom, rounded on the front edge, and narrow at the back. Because of this shape, there is less air pressure on the top of the wing. The greater pressure under the wing pushes upward and keeps the plane from falling.

OUCH!

Who Was King Arthur?

Arthur, an English king, is believed to have lived in the 6th century. No one is absolutely sure, but the legends about him are fantastic. They say that he was the only man to withdraw a magical sword from a stone. His Knights of the Roundtable included Sir Lancelot and Sir Galahad, the greatest soldiers in Europe. And he was supposedly handsome, courageous, and honest. It would be nice to know he really existed.

What's the star nearest to Earth?

Don't wait for dark to find it. Don't even take out your telescope. It's our very own daytime star, the sun, just 93 million miles away. The next closest star is Proxima Centauri, and it's 25 trillion miles from Earth.

WHAT IS ACID RAIN?

It's worse than bad weather. It's rain carrying chemical pollution. When industries burn coal and oil, sulfur and nitrogen rise into the air and dissolve in the atmosphere. When moisture forms, these chemicals become part of the water vapor that falls to the Earth as rain.

COUGH! COUGH!

WHAT WAS THE WORLD'S FIRST DOG?

I KNEW HIM WELL!

A wolf-like creature. The wolf is a member of the scientific family Canidae, which developed about 20 million years ago. All dogs are related to this same ancestor and are part of the same family. But today, there are many different dogs because of *selective breeding*. People have bred dogs with certain characteristics until a whole line of descendants developed. Now the world has big dogs and small, long and short-haired, pointy and floppy-eared, making the tiny Chihuahua and huge St. Bernard strange, but true relatives.

I FLEW BEFORE THEM!

WHO INVENTED THE FIRST POWERED AIRCRAFT?

The Wright brothers, Orville and Wilbur. When their biplane (a plane with two sets of wings) rose above the ground at Kitty Hawk, North Carolina, in 1903, it was the first flight powered by an engine. First it bumped along, but on the fourth try, Wilbur was airborne for 59 seconds and flew 852 feet.

WHO WAS THE ORIGINAL DRACULA?

The main character in an 1897 novel by Englishman Bram Stoker. The author based his story "on a king Vlad Dracula," who lived in the 1400s in Wallachia, a part of Romania. He was better known as Vlad the Impaler for his nasty habit of sticking the bodies of his enemies on wooden stakes like a fence. He is said to have once impaled 20,000 people as a warning to the invading Turks.

I CAN'T STAY... I'M LATE FOR LUNCH!

FEET DO YOUR THING!!

I'D RATHER SEE THE MOVIE!!

HOW DO EARTHWORMS HELP THE GROUND?

They make the ground good for plants. Creeping and crawling, earthworms loosen up the soil so plants can wiggle their roots down. Also, by leaving waste behind, earthworms fertilize the ground for growing plants.

WHAT MAKES ICE CUBES CRACK WHEN YOU PUT THEM IN A DRINK?

I HEARD THAT!

A temperature clash. When the ice cube meets the liquid, its outside begins to warm up and expand. But its icy center remains frozen and unmoved. Pressure between the outer, expanding part of the cube and its frozen center builds up until...*snap!*—the ice cube cracks.

What kinds of instruments are in a symphony orchestra?

LET'S BEGIN.

A ONE AND A TWO AND A THREE!

WAIT FOR ME!

I'M READY!

The sound of a symphony is a mix of these: *percussion*, like the drums and cymbals; *brass*, like the trumpet and trombone; *woodwind*, like the flute and clarinet; and *strings*, like the violin and cello. Ninety to 120 players put it all together—and the result is sweet music.

LET'S EAT!

WHY DO MY CHEEKS GET RED IN THE WINTER?

It's warm blood coming to the rescue of your cold skin. In winter, you wear a hat, coat, and gloves but probably not a face mask. So your body, all on its own, sends more rosy, warm blood to the vessels under your cheeks. It protects your face from frostbite.

WHO ATE THE FIRST SANDWICH?

Someone who was too busy to use silverware. The honor goes to an Englishman named, of course, the Earl of Sandwich. In the 1700s, he put some food between two slices of bread, took a bite, and made history.

What do red giants, white dwarves, and black holes have in common?

Stardom. But not the Hollywood type. Having burned off most of their helium and hydrogen fuel, they are all stars nearing the end of their existence. The dying star first swells and becomes a red giant. Then its enormous gravitational force shrinks it down into a white dwarf, still giving off some light. But a black hole does not. If the star is massive enough, its gravitational pull is so strong that even light can't escape its surface.

WHY DO POLICE USE FINGERPRINTS TO TRACE PEOPLE?

Because the pattern of lines on the underside of your fingertips is yours alone. And they're the same for your whole life. The lines are called loops, whorls, and arches. No two people have the same pattern— even identical twins have different fingerprints.

Hot-Air Balloons

Want a quiet ride? Try a balloon. Hot-air balloons float when the air inside the balloon is heated. The heated air is lighter than the cool air outside, so the balloon rises toward the sky. Once released, the balloon will float as high as its weight allows. Then the pilot must throw weight off to go higher, or release air to descend.

HAVE A NICE FLIGHT!

HELICOPTERS

Want to hang out? Take a helicopter ride. Helicopters can hover, or hang in the air, over one spot. The *rotor blades* above the cockpit are the "wings" that provide the lift and the direction. At a certain speed, the blades hold the helicopter in one spot. At a faster speed, the blades will lift it higher. Tilted, they send the aircraft backward, forward, and sideways. A small rotor on the tail completes the balancing act.

JET PLANE

Want to travel fast? Take a jet plane. The jet engine is called a turbofan. Fans at the front of the engine suck air into a compression chamber, where it is mixed with fuel and fired. The heated, high-pressure air and the exhaust gases rush out the back of the engine and thrust the plane forward. The first jet plane took off in 1947.

IT'S GETTING CROWDED UP HERE!

WE'RE HEADING FOR THE MOON!

WOW!

Airship

Want to travel light? Fly by airship. An airship is a cabin carried by a huge balloon filled with *helium*, a gas seven times lighter than air. The rising or *upthrust* of this balloon is so powerful that it can carry an engine, along with cabin and passengers. Small propellers and a rudder do the steering. Early airships carried as many as 200 people, but today's are usually the smaller variety—the blimp.

ROCKET

Want to blast off? Ride a rocket. A rocket is a heat engine with solid or liquid fuel, called a *propellant*. The basic principle of a rocket is the same as a firecracker. A highly flammable substance is packed into a chamber and fired. The hot gases that result stream out from the base and drive the rocket upward. It takes five huge rockets to shoot a space shuttle into orbit.

Who was Leonardo da Vinci?

THAT'S ME!

A genius. Leonardo (1452–1519) lived during the Italian Renaissance, a great artistic period. He is famous as a painter, and his work, the *Mona Lisa* is one of the most valuable paintings in the world. But he was also a scientist, inventor, engineer, architect, and designer. He made brilliant observations that paved the way for future scientists and inventors.

WHAT'S FOR LUNCH?

HOW DO PLANTS EAT?

They make food. They cook up sugars using the process of *photosynthesis*, which combines sunlight, carbon dioxide, and water from the soil. *Chlorophyll*, a green pigment which captures the sun's energy, makes this possible. Some plants that can't get what they need from the soil dine on insects. They capture them with sticky leaves—or petals that snap together like jaws.

I'M THE DRUMMER BOY.

WHY DO SOLDIERS SALUTE?

It's a military rule. A salute is a sign of respect to a person of higher rank. Bowing or kneeling to royalty or officers has gone on throughout history. A hand-to-the-forehead salute probably comes from taking off a hat as a gesture of respect—which may have come from the way knights removed their helmets when speaking to nobles.

I-I-I'M C-C-COLD!

WHAT IS THE LARGEST ORGAN IN MY BODY?

THE LAYER THAT PROTECTS ALL OF YOU—YOUR SKIN. AN ADULT MAN HAS ABOUT 20 SQUARE FEET OF SKIN, A WOMAN, 17 SQUARE FEET. (THAT'S IF IT WERE TAKEN OFF AND LAID OUT TO MEASURE.) SKIN FLAKES OFF ALL THE TIME. IT TAKES ABOUT A MONTH FOR NEW TISSUE TO REPLACE OLD.

When was the first zipper zipped?

In 1893, but it didn't stay closed for long. This first version, for boots and shoes, didn't work well. In 1913, Gideon Sundback invented a zipper that stayed zipped. Nobody cared until World War I in 1917, when zippers began appearing on military uniforms. Still, it wasn't until 1938 that the zipper replaced the buttons on men's pants.

IS EARTH GETTING WARMER?

That depends. Over the long term, Earth has gone from warmer to colder and back again. In dinosaur times, more than 65 million years ago, there were no ice caps at the poles, while during the Ice Age, 18,000 years ago, vast glaciers covered parts of the globe.

Over the short term, however, Earth *has* been getting warmer. Since the 19th century, Earth's average surface temperature has been rising—by 0.5°F in the past 25 years alone.

Who invented the ice-cream cone?

Italo Marcioni. He got a patent for a special cone mold in 1896. But ice cream didn't really meet cone in a big way until 1904 at the St. Louis Fair. An ice-cream vendor was next to a waffle maker. One rolled up a waffle—the other put ice cream in it. The rest is history.

What makes whirlpools whirl?

GULP!

Water that flows in a certain direction is called a current. When two currents collide, the force forms a swirl of water. Currents whipped by the wind, pulled by the tides, and interrupted by rocks can also form whirlpools. Some are powerful enough to suck down whatever gets caught in the middle.

HOW DO THE HOLES GET INTO SWISS CHEESE?

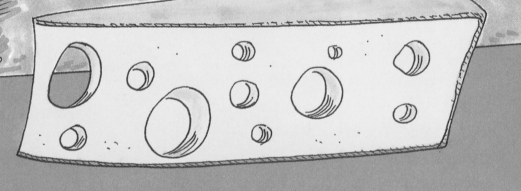

Bacteria puts them there. Cheese is a food whose flavor and texture is created by bacteria. The holes in Swiss cheese are made by "bubbles" of gas given off by its busy builders.

WHAT IS THE WORLD'S MOST POPULOUS CITY?

Tokyo, Japan. In 2005, Tokyo's metropolitan area – the city and its adjacent areas – had a population of 35 million people.

HOW DOES A LIGHT BULB LIGHT UP?

With a de*light*ful combination of electricity, metal, heat, and gas. Inside a bulb is a thin filament (wire) of tungsten, a metal with a very high melting point. That means it can take a lot of heat without melting. Electrical current heats the filament (as high as 4,500 degrees!) so that it glows with light. The bulb is airtight and filled with an inactive gas called argon, which keeps oxygen out and helps the bulb last longer.

WHAT ARE ROBOTS USED FOR?

Robots are good at doing the same task over and over again, exactly the same way. All robots are machines that have computer instructions built in. They paint cars. They lift heavy loads. They enter radioactive or hot areas too dangerous for humans. Some are simply arms and a gripper, with humans controlling them from a distance.

WHAT IS

MIRROR

GAS FILLED TUBE

ELECTRODE

ELECTRODE

SEMI-SILVERED MIRROR

How does a compact disc player work?

It uses laser light and a computer to change codes into sounds. Under its surface, a disc has tiny parts arranged in patterns in circular tracks. These patterns are computer coded and there are 600 million on a disc! As the disc spins, a laser light reads the patterns, sending electrical signals to a computer. The player's computer has a memory of all the possible signals, and turns the code into sounds.

WHAT ARE X RAYS?

Rays of energy similar to light rays. But unlike light, they travel *through* you. When an X ray is taken, the rays penetrate your body and strike a piece of photographic film. The result is a shadow picture of your insides. Denser parts, like bones, are brighter because they absorb X rays. Fleshy parts are dimmer because the rays pass through them.

A LASER?

A very intense beam of light. Lasers are created when the molecules of gases, liquids, or solids are so excited by electricity that they burst into a single, concentrated, powerful stream of light. Some cut through steel or drill holes in diamonds. Others perform everyday tasks. They play audio discs and read the bar codes on groceries.

IS THERE LIFE ON OTHER PLANETS?

TAKE ME TO YOUR LEADER.

Not likely in our solar sytem. Certainly no creatures with melon heads and almond eyes. No little green men. The other planets don't have atmospheres that could support life as we know it on Earth. And their temperatures are extreme—too hot or too cold. We know the moon has no life because we've been there. And space probes have found no life on Mars. But there may be planets similar to Earth revolving around some of the billions and billions of stars in outer space.

WHO CREATED THE ALPHABET?

For thousands of years people drew pictures, creating a symbol—like a drawing of the sun—to stand for an object or an idea. The ancient Egyptians and other Middle Eastern peoples were the first to communicate this way. That was about 5,000 years ago. About 3,000 years ago, the Greeks had a complete alphabet. The Greek alphabet was further changed by the Romans in the first century A.D. It's the Roman alphabet that English is based on. You can see the history in the word "alphabet." It comes from the first two letters of the Greek alphabet, alpha and beta.

Do all birds sing?

No. Most birds make some kind of sound, but bird-song is different from calls, squawks, chattering, or caws. Among the various species known as songbirds, males are usually the only ones that sing. They do it to let females know that they are available for mating. Sometimes, they sing to let other males know that they are claiming a certain territory.

WHERE WERE THE FIRST OLYMPICS HELD?

Olympia, Greece. The ancient Greek Olympics, held over 2,000 years ago, are the inspiration for today's games. The Greeks ended their games in 393 B.C., and it wasn't until 1896 that the games began again as an international event. The world has missed only three dates, 1916, 1940, and 1944 because of the two world wars.

TO OLYMPICS

WANT TO RACE?

WHY ARE SO MANY PEOPLE RIGHT-HANDED?

Your brain decides. But there are still some things about the brain that scientists don't know—and this is one of them. Nine out of ten people are right-handed. Nobody knows why.

How can I get **SUNBURNED** on a cloudy day?

If it's daytime, the sun is out whether we can see it or not. The sun's energy reaches us mostly as heat and light, but 6% is ultraviolet radiation (UVR), which causes sunburn. Clouds and pollution block some UVR, but the sun's rays are so strong that dangerous amounts still reach us.

How do crickets make their sound?

They wing it. Crickets, like most insects, have no vocal chords. But they do have some things to say, like "Hello," or "Here I am." Crickets make a noise by rubbing the hard, ridged tips of their wings together. That's cricket communication, but it's music to *our* ears.

I DON'T PLAY CRICKET.

Why do the continents look as though they fit together like a jigsaw puzzle?

One theory is that the Earth was once a huge single land mass that broke up. Over millions of years, pieces slowly drifted apart and became the continents as we know them today. The continents and the oceans have gigantic plates beneath them that move very slowly. So the positions of the continents are always changing ever so slightly.

IT FITS!

Who invented ROCK 'N' ROLL?

It was born in the 1950s. It grew from rhythm and blues music played by African-American artists like Chuck Berry, Little Richard, and others. Combined with gospel, folk, and country and western music, it came together in a new sound. Elvis Presley sold millions of rock 'n' roll records and became known as the "King of Rock 'n' Roll." When the Beatles brought their music from England in the 1960s, rock 'n' roll was here to stay.

I DIDN'T KNOW THAT!

WHAT IS A MUMMY?

It's not necessarily what most people think of—an Egyptian corpse wrapped in cloth. When bacteria and fungi cannot grow in a dead body, it becomes *mummified*. A mummy still has some of the body's soft tissues (skin, muscles, or organs). Some mummies were made by *embalming*, which is any process used to preserve a dead body. Ancient Egyptians did this with linen and tree resin (sap) because they believed in preparing the body for life after death. However, humans and animals have been found naturally mummified all over the world, usually in very dry or very cold places.

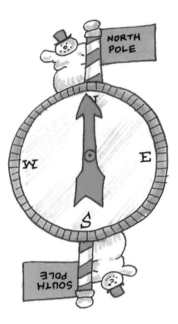

Why does a compass always point North?

THERE'S AN INVISIBLE, BUT NOT MYSTERIOUS, FORCE AT WORK. THE NEEDLE ON A COMPASS IS A THIN, FREELY SWINGING MAGNET. THE EARTH IS ALSO A GIANT MAGNET, WITH ITS NORTH AND SOUTH POLES NEAR THE NORTH AND SOUTH POLES ON THE MAP. THE NORTH POLE OF THE EARTH'S MAGNETIC FIELD ATTRACTS THE NORTH POLE OF THE NEEDLE, CAUSING IT TO POINT NORTH.

WHY DOES SOME SPOILED FOOD TURN GREEN?

It's the dreaded mold. Mold is all around us in the air and in the ground. It's a kind of fungus that grows in moist places, on food left out on the counter, and even on forgotten food in the back of the refrigerator. The tiny bits of mold grow into a large, green colony.

HOW OLD IS THE EARTH?

I FORGOT TO BUY A GIFT!

Very old—about 4.6 billion years. Primitive forms of life, like algae and bacteria, began to appear about a billion years later, when the planet developed the water and oxygen necessary to support living things. Fossils exist that show primitive life forms from 3.5 million years ago.

WHY DO I GET A SCAB WHEN I GET A CUT?

NICE MASK!

WHY DO PEOPLE DRESS IN COSTUMES ON HALLOWEEN?

To scare away the ghosts. In ancient times, the Celtic peoples of England prepared themselves for the dark days of winter with a festival. They lit bonfires and sacrificed animals. They expected evil spirits to be roaming about. To hide from them, they dressed up in costumes.

I'M NOT WEARING A MASK!

Who was Hans Christian Andersen?

HE WROTE ABOUT ME.

The man who wrote "The Ugly Duckling," "The Emperor's New Clothes," "The Princess and the Pea," and 165 other fairy tales. He was Danish, wrote during the 1800s, and told stories that still make us laugh and sigh today.

It's a natural bandage. Healthy blood cells come to the rescue of those torn by a cut. They thicken and clot, and add chemicals and other substances, which dry, shrink, and harden the cut cells. Then they become a scab—a seal that keeps blood in and germs out.

Why are some clouds white ...while others are gray or... black?

Because clouds are masses of water droplets and ice crystals. Sometimes shadows make clouds look gray. But usually, the more dense the water within a cloud, the grayer it is—and the sooner the rain.

IT'S NOT RAINING!

IT'S RAINING!

CAN ALL BIRDS FLY?

WHY SHOULD I FLY? I'M NOT GOING ANYWHERE!

Not big birds. Not the penguin, nor the ostrich. The shape of giant birds like the ostrich, the South American rhea, and the Australian emu keeps them from flying, as much as their weight does. Small birds have enormous breast muscles relative to the rest of their streamlined bodies that enable them to flap their wings and fly. Big birds don't.

WHERE IS THE WORLD'S LONGEST CAVE?

The Mammoth Cave and Flint Ridge cave system in Kentucky have many interconnected cave passages. Together, they form a system with an overall length of 348 miles—and counting!

WHAT IS A TSUNAMI?

A series of giant waves created by a violent shake-up of the ocean's floor, such as an earthquake or a volcanic eruption. Moving at an average of 450 miles an hour, these waves gain height and power. A *tsunami* (soo-NAH-mee) may be only three feet high in open sea, but may tower as high as 100 feet by the time it reaches land.

THAT'S *FAST!*

If the Earth is *moving,* why can't we feel it?

I DON'T FEEL A THING!

MAYBE THAT'S WHY I ACT DIZZY!!

Gravity keeps our feet on the ground. Even though Earth is spinning very fast—at about 1,083 miles per hour at the surface—we don't feel it. That is because we are on or close to Earth's surface, moving along at the same speed.

What's the difference between an alligator

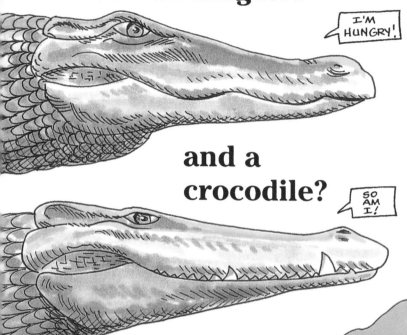

and a crocodile?

An alligator has a broader, rounder snout. A crocodile's snout is thinner and pointier. When a crocodile closes its mouth, the larger teeth on its bottom jaw rest in spaces on the **outside** of its upper jaw. In an alligator's mouth, they rest on the **inside** of the jaw.

HOW DO MOLES LIVE UNDERGROUND?

THEY CONSTANTLY DIG TUNNELS WITH THEIR STRONG FRONT CLAWS SEARCHING FOR TASTY WORMS AND GRUBS TO EAT. THE TUNNELS ALSO CONNECT THEM TO UNDERGROUND NESTS AND RESTING PLACES. THEIR MOLEHILLS, THE EXCESS EARTH FROM ALL THAT DIGGING, HAVE RUINED MANY A LAWN.

FOR RENT

How and why do chameleons change color?

It's hide-and-seek in the animal world every day. Some animals hide while others seek to eat them. The chameleon has a natural ability to hide by changing its colors to match its surroundings. If it stays long enough in one spot, its color cells will change to blend in with the background. They also change color when it's too hot or cold, or if they feel threatened.

Which water- fall has the most water?

Khone Falls, in Laos, a country in Asia. Its flow of 2.5 million gallons of water per second gives it the greatest volume of any waterfall in the world. That is nearly twice the volume of Niagara Falls, which has the greatest volume of any U.S. waterfall.

Why can I see myself in a mirror?

Everything you see comes from light rays that bounce off objects and bounce back to your eyes. A mirror is glass with a shiny chemical coating on the back. When you stand in front of a mirror, light rays bounce off your body onto the mirror's coating. Then the rays reflect, or bounce back, to your eyes. What you are is what you see—it's your reflection.

WHAT ARE SUNSPOTS?

They're cool. Sunspots are places on the surface of the sun caused by changes in the sun's magnetic field. The surface temperature of the sun is about 10,000°Fahrenheit. Sunspots are about 3,600 degrees cooler. But cool on the sun is still hot, hot, hot.

ARE PEOPLE REALLY WEIGHTLESS IN OUTER SPACE?

Yes, as long as they are in a zero-gravity environment—out of range of the gravity of a planet, moon, or other large body.

People who spend any length of time in space—on a space station, for example—suffer from the effects of weightlessness: They lose body weight as well as calcium from their bones. They usually get back to normal soon after returning to Earth.

WHERE IS THE LARGEST LIBRARY?

The United States Library of Congress in Washington, DC. Know what you want before you go there, because it contains over 100 million items. And don't get lost in the shelves—there are 575 miles of them. The first modern public library in the United States was in New Hampshire in 1833, and it had 700 books. The largest public library today is in Chicago, and it's stacked with 11.4 million books.

WHAT MAKES A VOLCANO *ERUPT?*

A volcano erupting is a...**BLAST!** that comes from below. Volcanoes are located in places where plates are shifting beneath the Earth's crust. In such spots, hot liquid rock (magma) and gases are trying to escape. Pressure from these elements builds up until . . . **WHOOSH!** . . . they shoot up the center of a volcano. Fire, smoke, and ashes leap into the sky and lava pours down the sides of the volcano.

I'M BLOWING MY TOP!

I'D HAVE MY OWN TV SERIES ···IF TV HAD BEEN INVENTED!

WHEN WAS THE FIRST PLAY PERFORMED?

A *long* time ago—around 500 B.C. The first dramatists were the Greeks. They wrote and performed tragedies—serious plays—as well as comedies to make people laugh. Some plays have survived and are still performed today! The ancient Greek plays are considered to be among the great literature of the world.

FUNNY!

SAD!

I HOPE THEY MAKE THE ICE SOFTER!

How does the ice in a skating rink keep from MELTING?

Watch your toes, the floor is freezing. Beneath the ice is a concrete floor with pipes that are filled with a freezing solution. An Olympic rink may have up to 11 miles of these chilling pipes. So the weather above doesn't affect the ice as much as the temperature below.

I DON'T ICE SKATE!

WHO WAS KING TUT?

Tutankhamen (toot-ang-KAH-men) was his name, and he has been called the "boy king" of Egypt. Tut became king in 1361 B.C. when he was only nine years old. He died when he was about 19. His tomb and its fabulous riches weren't discovered until 1922—3,000 years after he was buried. He was found in a coffin made from 2,500 pounds of gold!

IS THERE GOLD AT A RAINBOW'S END?

JUST KIDDING!

No such luck. That good-luck tale comes from Irish folklore, in which anyone who reached a rainbow's end would find a leprechaun's pot o' gold.

Not everyone considers a rainbow good luck. In ancient Greece, the word for rainbow was *iris*, named for the goddess of war and unrest. In one African folktale, a rainbow that touched one's house was a snake that brought bad luck.

HOW DOES AN ELECTRIC EEL MAKE ELECTRICITY?

Body batteries. Electric eels, and other fish like the torpedo ray and some catfish, have thousands of linked natural battery cells in a coat of muscle tissue. A six-foot-long South American electric eel can generate a 500-volt zap of electricity—enough to light up a dozen bulbs.

ARE WE RELATED?

HOW SHOCKING!

WHAT IS CORAL?

A coral *polyp* is a tiny ocean animal with a skeleton on the outside and a soft body inside. When the body dies, the skeleton remains. Some corals live in large colonies. Their skeletons, millions and millions of them, form *reefs*, a giant wall of coral in the sea not far from shore. Corals can be shaped like flowers, fans, fingers, or even giant brains.

WHY DON'T FISH SINK?

Many fish have an organ called a swim bladder that helps keep them afloat. A fish remains balanced by changing the amount of air in its swim bladder, which is something like a balloon. Fish take in air from the water around them as it flows in through their gills.

HOW DOES A COMPUTER THINK?

It doesn't. Computers *operate*. They do amazing things, but not without instructions. A computer has four basic units: memory, input, central processing, and output. The **memory** holds programs that tell the computer how to perform different tasks (play games, process words, add numbers, etc.). The **input** unit (keyboard) provides the information (data) that the program will work on. The **processing unit** uses the data to follow the program and work out results. The **output** unit displays the results—on a screen or through a printer.

I DON'T WRITE LETTERS!

EVERYONE WRITES LETTERS!

WHEN WAS THE FIRST POSTAGE STAMP USED?

In 1840 in Great Britain. Queen Victoria's picture was printed on over 60 million stamps called "Penny Blacks." George Washington and Benjamin Franklin were given the same honor in the United States seven years later. Many people collect stamps. One of the first British Penny Blacks was sold in 1991 for over $2 million.

WHERE DOES **CHOCOLATE** COME FROM?

Most people don't care as long as they can eat it, chew it, drink it, or let it melt in their mouths. The cocoa tree and its bean are the source of chocolate. When the beans are melted down, they become liquid cocoa. **DO NOT** drink it. It's so bitter it puckers up your mouth. Lots of sugar is added before it becomes chocolate.

How can a scientist tell how old a fossil is?

Radioactivity—it goes on and on. Mineralized fossils give off small amounts of nuclear radioactivity. The radioactivity slowly decreases over thousands and thousands of years. So scientists can take a bone, measure the changes in radioactivity, and tell how long ago the plant or animal lived.

Why do leaves turn colors in the fall?

For the tree's survival. Trees must shed their leaves to conserve water during the winter. So a film forms where the leaf joins the tree, cutting off food. That's when the colors change. Chlorophyll, which makes the leaf green, begins to break down. All the other colors—yellow, red, gold, and purple—which were hidden by the green, begin to show.

WHY DOES THE MOON CHANGE SHAPE IN THE SKY?

It doesn't. Only what we *see* changes. The moon circles the entire Earth about once every month. The moon reflects the sun's light. As it travels, we see the whole moon or parts of it, depending on where we are on Earth. These are the moon's *phases*, from a curved sliver to a full moon and back again.

I'M THE ALARM CLOCK FOR THIS FARM.

Why do roosters crow in the morning?

It's their mating call. Roosters crow to attract females. They learned to crow when the light was dim—early morning and just before dark so their enemies were less likely to see them.

Who was Sitting Bull?

A fierce Native American leader, who tried to keep settlers from taking the land of his people, the Sioux. In 1876, Sitting Bull led nearly 2,000 warriors in one of the greatest defeats of American troops—the Battle of Little Bighorn.

I HEAR A ROOSTER CROWING!

JUST CALL ME SPEEDY!

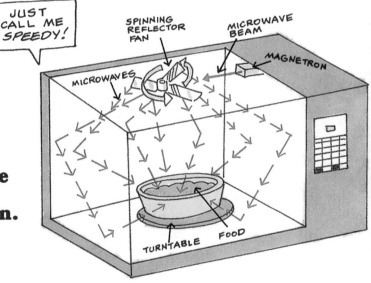

SPINNING REFLECTOR FAN

MICROWAVE BEAM

MAGNETRON

MICROWAVES

TURNTABLE   FOOD

HOW DOES A MICROWAVE OVEN WORK?

Fast. In a microwave oven, a strong electrical current is changed into tiny *micro* waves. These radiate inside the oven, pass right through the food, bounce off the walls, and zip through the food again. The inside and outside are cooked all at once. In a regular oven, heat waves hit the outside of food and slowly cook inward.

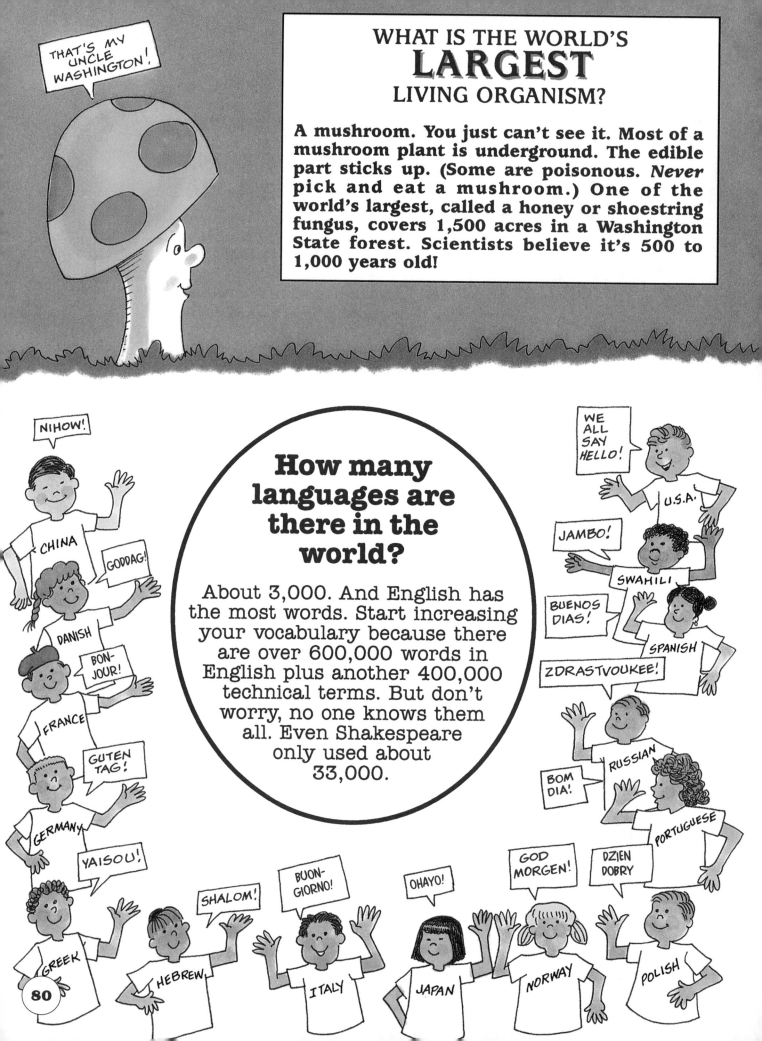

WHAT IS THE WORLD'S LARGEST LIVING ORGANISM?

A mushroom. You just can't see it. Most of a mushroom plant is underground. The edible part sticks up. (Some are poisonous. *Never* pick and eat a mushroom.) One of the world's largest, called a honey or shoestring fungus, covers 1,500 acres in a Washington State forest. Scientists believe it's 500 to 1,000 years old!

THAT'S MY UNCLE WASHINGTON!

How many languages are there in the world?

About 3,000. And English has the most words. Start increasing your vocabulary because there are over 600,000 words in English plus another 400,000 technical terms. But don't worry, no one knows them all. Even Shakespeare only used about 33,000.

NIHOW! — CHINA
GODDAG! — DANISH
BONJOUR! — FRANCE
GUTEN TAG! — GERMANY
YAISOU! — GREEK
SHALOM! — HEBREW
BUONGIORNO! — ITALY
OHAYO! — JAPAN
GOD MORGEN! — NORWAY
DZIEN DOBRY — POLISH
WE ALL SAY HELLO! — U.S.A.
JAMBO! — SWAHILI
BUENOS DIAS! — SPANISH
ZDRASTVOUKEE! — RUSSIAN
BOM DIA! — PORTUGUESE

WHY DOES A GIRAFFE HAVE SUCH A LONG NECK?

Animal traits develop over thousands of years. The ones that last are characteristics that help them eat well and avoid enemies. A long neck gives the giraffe two important advantages. It can eat the leaves on the tops of trees that other animals can't reach. And it can see enemies coming from a long way off.

I COULD PLAY PRO BASKETBALL!

Why do I need sleep?

Get up—Go to school—Eat—Run around—Think—Throw a ball. Your body is working all day long. Waste builds up and slows down your systems. It makes you feel tired. Sleep is the time when your body cleans up, repairs, and relaxes. You must sleep. How much? Only your body knows.

WHEN DID PEOPLE START EATING WITH KNIVES AND FORKS?

Knives were the first tool for killing *and* eating. During dinner, people cut their food with a knife and ate it with their hands. Forks came into use in Italy in the 1500s when fancy-dressed people found their lacy sleeves trailing in the mashed potatoes. In 1699, the king of France started the tradition of using knives with rounded ends.

WHO BUILT THE TAJ MAHAL AND WHY?

The magnificent Taj Mahal in northern India is a mausoleum, or tomb, built by the emperor Shah Jahan in memory of his wife. The mausoleum gets its name from *her* name, Mumtaz Mahal, which means "ornament of the palace." Twenty thousand men worked for over 20 years to build the complex, which includes several buildings, a reflecting pool, and a walled garden. The square tomb (186 feet on each side) has white marble walls, decorated with semiprecious stones, and is topped by five marble domes. The building was completed in 1648. Shah Jahan is also buried there.

HOW DO PEANUTS GROW?

Upside down. "Nuts" are really the seeds of the plant they come from. Most plants grow up toward the sun. But not the nutty peanut plant. Its seed pods grow downward and bury themselves in the soil. Then the peanut ripens underground.

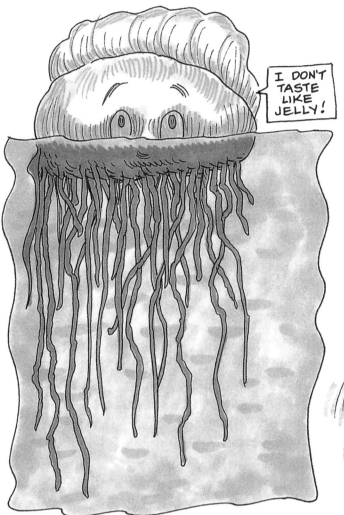

WHAT ARE JELLYFISH?

They're not really fish, because they don't have backbones. Jellyfish are undersea creatures with tentacles and a jelly-like body shaped like an upside down cup. The sting you feel in the water is the poison a jellyfish releases to catch prey. The Portuguese man-of-war has tentacles that can be more than 100 feet long. It can produce very painful stings if touched by a human.

WHY DO MY MUSCLES ACHE WHEN I EXERCISE A LOT?

Bend your elbow, clench your fist, and make a muscle in your arm. Feel the muscle get rounder and firmer? Now let go. Feel it stretch and relax? When you *contract* and *relax* a muscle, the tissues produce lactic acid. That creates the achy, tired feeling you get. Rest, and you're ready to go again.

HOW DO FIREWORKS WORK?

All that dazzle, flash, and sparkle is chemistry in motion. A firecracker is a two-staged event set off by gunpowder, chemicals, and a fuse. Light a firecracker and the gunpowder sends it flying. Then the fuse ignites the chemicals—and pow—strontium burns red; barium, green; copper, blue; and sodium, yellow. But remember, all that beauty is dangerous. Keep your hands *off!*

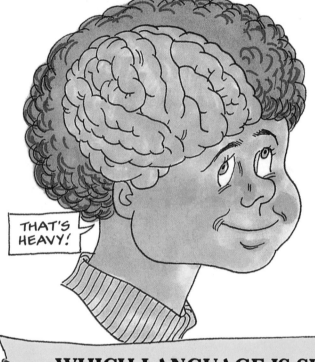

THAT'S HEAVY!

HOW MUCH DOES MY BRAIN WEIGH?

About 2% of your body weight. That's two pounds if you weigh 100. But the brain needs about ten times more of your body's resources— 20% of the oxygen you breathe, 20% of the calories in the food you eat, and 15% of the blood you have. Your busy brain needs lots of fuel to keep you going.

WHICH LANGUAGE IS SPOKEN BY THE MOST PEOPLE IN THE WORLD?

English. But, check the numbers. For many people, English is a second language. Estimates range from 800 million to 1.5 billion English speakers in the world. But English is the *native tongue* of only 350 million. Of those, 220 million live in North America. Mandarin Chinese is the most common *first language*, shared by close to a billion people.

THANK YOU!

SHIEH-SHIEH!

HOW DO MIGRATING BIRDS KNOW WHERE THEY ARE GOING?

They probably follow the same guides used by sailors of ancient times: the stars, the sun, and geographic features such as shorelines and mountains. Some scientists think that birds also use Earth's magnetic fields to help them find their way, but this theory has not been proven. Most migrating birds use specific north-south routes called flyways.

WHO FIRST STARTED USING MAKEUP?

Japanese actors, African dancers, Egyptian princesses, and Roman empresses. Makeup has been around since ancient times. Over two thousand years ago Cleopatra, the queen of Egypt, blackened her upper eyelids and lashes and put dark green color under her eyes. Red was the color of choice for cheeks and lips in Rome. What's new today? Not much—just more brands and colors to choose from.

HOW OFTEN DO TIDES CHANGE?

Four times a day. In any given place, two low tides and two high tides usually occur each day.

The time of each tide varies slightly from day to day. Using knowledge of an area's shoreline, sea depth, and other factors, experts draw up tide charts that list the times of the tides for specific dates. Sailors and other people who live or work near seacoasts use the charts to help them plan anything that would be affected by the water's depth.

I DO IT!

HI, GUYS!

IT'S HIGH TIDE!

IT'S LOW TIDE!

HOW MANY BONES ARE IN MY BODY?

Adults have 206. You had about 275 when you were born. As you grow some smaller bones fuse together to form larger, stronger ones. More than half your bones are in your hands and feet. Your thigh bone, or femur, is the largest. The ossicles, inside your ears, are the smallest. Bones protect your organs. And the marrow in the center of bones produces the red and white blood cells you need to live.

IS THAT ME ?

Why do camels have humps? How long can a camel go without water?

WILL YOU BRING ME A GLASS OF WATER, PLEASE?

Camels are built for long, dry journeys. Their humps are for fat storage. When food is short, they use up the fat for energy. Their stomach lining is specially built for water storage. How long camels can go without a drink depends on their travel speed and the weight of the load they're carrying. It's about 6 to 10 days if traveling is slow and easy.

Who kept the world's longest diary?

A very old person. Colonel Ernest Loftus, of Zimbabwe, began writing in his diary when he was 12 years old. He kept it up for 91 years until he died in 1987. He was 103.

Why do flowers have such bright colors?

To attract the birds and the bees so the flowers can be pollinated (fertilized) and produce seeds. Most flowers rely on insects and birds to carry their pollen. The visitors brush against the pollen and carry it on their bodies from one part of the flower to another, or from one flower to another.

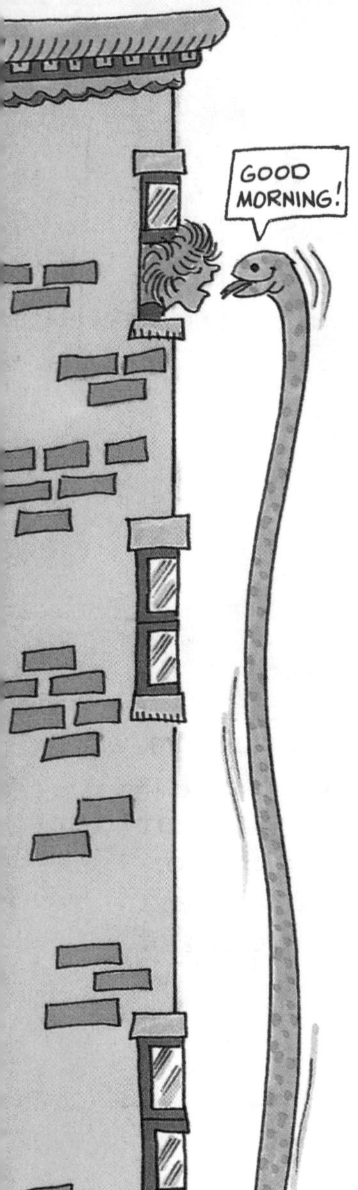

HOW LONG CAN A SNAKE GET?

If the snake could stand on its tail and you were at a window on the third story of a building, about 30 feet up, the snake could look you in the eye! This long, *long* snake could be an anaconda or a reticulated python, but fortunately, both stick to the ground.

GOOD MORNING!

THE SURF'S UP!

WAY TO GO!

ALL ABOARD

THIS IS FUN!

I FORGOT MY WET-SUIT!

WHO INVENTED SURFING?

People began surfing before anyone thought to record it. Hawaiians were catching waves when Captain Cook discovered the islands in 1778. They used big, heavy boards in those days. When smaller, lightweight boards were invented in the 1930s, surfing took off.

I USED TO SURF.

?

SPEED OF LIGHT?

Incredibly fast—faster than anyone can imagine. Light travels at a speed of about 186,000 miles per second. The circumference of the Earth (the distance around the world) is about 24,800 miles. That means light could travel around the world about seven and a half times in a single second!

DO YOU WANT TO RACE?

OKAY!

WHAT INSECT FLIES THE FASTEST?

The dragonfly. When a dragonfly comes by, duck! It can travel as fast as 30 miles per hour. But compared to many insects, this big bug beats its wings slowly—only about 25 to 40 beats per second. When a tiny mosquito takes off, it beats its wings (buzzzz!) about 600 beats per second, but only travels about one mile per hour.

DRAW ME!

Who was Walt Disney?

Mickey Mouse's "father." Disney (1901–1966) was a famous filmmaker. One of his earliest and most well-known creations was Mickey Mouse. In 1928, Mickey starred in Disney's first sound cartoon, *Steamboat Willie*, and Disney was his voice.

Disney created the first full-length cartoon, *Snow White and the Seven Dwarfs*, in 1937. He built Disneyland theme park in California in 1955. Disneyworld, near Orlando, Florida, was opened in 1971.

INDEX